LINES & RHYMES

THE POET SHERIFF,
Frank J. Anderson

© 2022 Frank J. Anderson. All rights reserved.

No part of this book may be reproduced, stored in a retrieval system, or transmitted by any means without the written permission of the author.

AuthorHouse™
1663 Liberty Drive
Bloomington, IN 47403
www.authorhouse.com
Phone: 833-262-8899

Because of the dynamic nature of the Internet, any web addresses or links contained in this book may have changed since publication and may no longer be valid. The views expressed in this work are solely those of the author and do not necessarily reflect the views of the publisher, and the publisher hereby disclaims any responsibility for them.

This book is printed on acid-free paper.

ISBN: 978-1-6655-4749-9 (sc)
ISBN: 978-1-6655-4750-5 (e)

Library of Congress Control Number: 2021925318

Print information available on the last page.

Published by AuthorHouse rev. date 01/10/2022

Sheriff Frank J. Anderson

A Poet With A Lifetime in Public Safety

From the Navy Shore Patrol to the Marion County Sheriff's Office, Frank Anderson has spent an entire lifetime as a peace officer protecting his fellow citizens, enforcing our nation's laws, and keeping our families and neighborhoods safe. Anderson was elected Marion County Sheriff on November 5, 2002, by a very sizable majority. Anderson was overwhelmingly re-elected in 2006, and served as the first head of the Indianapolis Metropolitan Police Department.

Previously, Frank Anderson served his country for more than 23 years in the U.S. Marshal's Service, one of the oldest and most prestigious law enforcement agencies in the nation. Anderson served as U.S. Marshal for the Southern District of Indiana, the chief federal law enforcement official in more than half of Indiana, first from 1977 to 1981, and again from 1994 to 2001. As U.S. Marshal, Anderson oversaw federal law enforcement for 62 Indiana counties with offices in Indianapolis, Evansville, Terre Haute and New Albany. He was responsible for pursuing and arresting federal fugitives, managing assets seized from criminal operations, and protecting federal witnesses and federal judges. In 2001, Anderson received the *Martin J. Burke Award*, given to the most outstanding Marshal in the entire nation.

Before his appointment as Marshal, Frank Anderson served 12 years in the Marshal's Service, first as a Deputy Marshal, and later as an Inspector and Security Specialist. He helped found and later direct the U.S. Federal Witness Protection Program. Anderson also worked organized crime cases, numerous undercover assignments and various other sensitive details.

From 1983 to 1994, Frank Anderson was district director of the Federal Protective Service for the U.S. General Service Administration. There he was in charge of security at federal-owned and leased facilities in Indiana and Minnesota and parts of Wisconsin and Illinois. Before his appointment as District Director, Anderson founded Unified Securities Associates, his own investigative and security service.

Sheriff Anderson grew up in Indianapolis and graduated from Shortridge High School, where he was an avid student-athlete. In fact, Sheriff Anderson's outstanding career in high school wrestling earned him induction into the Indiana Wrestling Hall of Fame. He began his career in law enforcement in 1956 in the U.S. Navy as a Shore Patrol officer and was honorably discharged in 1959. From 1961 to 1965, Anderson served as a Marion County Sheriff's Deputy. He has been married for more than 50 years to Mary Mercedes Anderson and has two grown children and three grandchildren. In 2019, Frank J. Anderson was awarded an Honorary Doctorate of Laws Degree by Martin University in recognition of a life devoted to upholding the rule of law.

*****

LR10348.0975405 4833-1555-3051v1

My Life Goals

My goals throughout my life and careers was to use my
God given abilities and experiences to make my
Communities, my Country and the World a better place for
all of us to live in peace with each other.

Frank J. Anderson

SOMETHING TO THINK ABOUT

BY FRANK J. ANDERSON
WRITTEN JANUARY 20, 2009

TODAY I WITNESSED THE SWEARING IN OF OUR FIRST BLACK PRESIDENT.
I HAD NO RESERVATIONS AS TO WHAT IT MEANT.
WITH MY 90-YEAR OLD FATHER AT MY SIDE.
WE BOTH CRIED WITH UNDERSTANDABLE PRIDE.
IN OUR WILDEST IMAGINATION.
DID WE EVER THINK, WE WOULD SEE A BLACK MAN LEAD OUR NATION?
MY FATHER AND I WITNESSED, AND WERE VICTIMS OF HATRED IN PARTS OF OUR NATION.
BUT THROUGH IT ALL IT HAS TAKEN EXTREME PATIENCE.
THE PROMISE TO MAKE A BETTER LIFE FOR ALL OF US.
LIES WITHIN OUR PERSONAL TRUST.
AS PRESIDENT OBAMA REPEATEDLY SAID, "YES WE CAN".
THERE IS NO DOUBT THAT HE IS THE RIGHT MAN.
WE HAVE COME A LONG WAY FOR THE PROMISE OF THIS DAY
BUT FOR IT TO BE REAL, WE MUST CONTINUE TO PRAY. DR. KING SAID "NOW IS THE TIME".
"NOW IS THE TIME THAT WE MUST LEARN TO LIVE TOGETHER AS BROTHERS AND SISTERS, OR SURELY WE WILL DIE AS FOOLS."
YES, PRESIDENT OBAMA, "YES WE CAN".
"NOW IS THE TIME". THAT ALL RACES MUST JOIN HAND IN HAND.
TO SUPPORT THIS VERY SPECIAL MAN.
I FEEL THE PRESENCE OF MY MOTHER ON THIS DAY
THAT IS SOMETHING THAT NO ONE CAN EVER TAKE AWAY.
THE DREAM IS STILL ALIVE, BUT IT IS TIME TO AWAKEN.
NOT QUITE COMPLETELY "FREE AT LAST".
BUT LET US LEAVE ALL OUR NEGATIVES IN THE PAST.
I AM CONFIDENT THAT SOME DAY, DR. KING'S DREAM WILL COME TRUE.
BUT IT WILL TAKE ALL OF US TO SEE IT THROUGH.
THE REST OF OUR JOURNEY MAY BE DIFFICULT THROUGH OUR LIFE.
LET US NOT FORGET THOSE WHO HAVE MADE THE SUPREME SACRIFICE.
"NOW IS THE TIME"
"YES WE CAN."

Is It Me or Is It You?

By Frank J. Anderson
April 18, 2018

As I sat in this chair today
I find myself without much to say

I try to have a quiet moment
But trouble is all up on it

It comes from the left and the right
And makes me want to fight

But something from deep within
Say that it is not the way to win

I have to turn to the belief that
I am accustomed to from within

It always turns hate into love
That comes from above

I am being given a test of my Faith
I will not turn it into waste

This is a personal challenge to me
That no one else can see

This moment that I must go through
Is something that I have to do

The feelings that I am going through
May also be happening to you

I will endeavor to see what I must do
But your part is up to you

I will endeavor not to have this feeling forever
It is up to you if we make this a joint endeavor

You and I must be truthful as to
Who, when, and why made us cry

A Simple Rule

By Frank J. Anderson
04/10/21

If you have conflict with your God-given sister or brother in passing.

Do you walk away, or do You stay?

The decision that you make,

if wrong, is a mistake.

Everyone wants to win, when there is confrontation.

Confrontation with each other, divides the nation.

It says in the Good Book "Those who control their anger have great understanding,

Those with a hasty temper will make mistakes."

Mistakes bring about heartaches and hate.

STOP and THINK before it's too late!

"Those who are short tempered do foolish things and are hated."

The next time you have confrontation,

Put your anger on vacation.

To: Pops

By Frank J. Anderson

Dear Pops, we know you have left us on this day.

But, I truly know you have gone to pave OUR way.

Who are we to say when it's time to go.

You have always been the person in the know.

We will shed many tears.

But, Oh what wonderful years

We have had, you as my Dad.

You have picked us up when we were down.

That is why God has given you a crown.

Thanks for the love and wisdom you have given us.

We promise that we will not make a fuss.

It will be difficult here without you.

But, we know you will be watching over us, and see us through.

Some day we will see you on the other side.

We promise you that will be a day of pride.

We have many decisions to make each day.

We need your help along the way.

You have taught us to work together and get along.

In doing so, no one will do wrong.

We know that Mama is by your side.

That gives us all tremendous pride.

You were number one, the tops.

This is why we love you Pops.

Frank J. Anderson

Stop and Think

By Frank J. Anderson
June 11, 2018

This message is to all my young brothers and sisters
As you go forward in your life and receive advice from others
Take a good look at the person who is giving it to you
If there is no good to it, don't do it
Everyone wants to be liked, and popular
But remember crime can be a life stopper
You must "Stop and Think" before making critical decisions in life,
Whether you are a girl or boy
The continuation of your life is not a toy
To bring a child into the world at your young age would be a big mistake,
"Stop and Think"
I say if there is no good to it don't do it. If it is a sin, it could be the end
You must practice the 5P's in life, "Proper Planning Prevents Poor Performance"
When physically challenged by others
You must "Stop and Think" again who's going to win, or could this be the end
The result of your actions could have negative effects on you
and your love ones and others
An alternative to "Confrontation" is "Hesitation" and not "Participation"
The mistake you make today may follow you for the rest of your life, again you
must "Stop and Think"
Your education must be completed without hesitation
Follow the 5P's and you will see and agree
My remarks come to you from my nearly 80 years of life experiences
having practiced these remarks to you
Best of luck, the world is waiting for you

A Few Thoughts

by Frank J. Anderson

This is the moment that I take the time to say these things to you.
Most of them I thought you knew.

How many times do I have to say I love you.
Most of the time, I thought you knew.

If I tell you from time to time that I love you.
In my opinion that should see us through.

It is not that I don't want to say that that each and every day.
It is just my way.

From time to time as I go through each day.
I sometimes don't know what to say.

For the thoughts that I have for you in my heart,
will always be there and never part.

You are always reminding me that I don't say certain things to you.
It is not because I don't know what to do.

After all the years that we have been through,
I hope you will continue to know that I love you.

I would hope there is **never** a doubt.
If there is, we will **always** work it out.

As we go through the rest of our days,
I hope we never part ways.

So as we go forward from this day on,
I promise you that you'll never be alone.

Things We Need To Do

By Frank J. Anderson

I know the history of where and how our Nation Begins.
But, I don't want to see it end.

There is a continued fight,
between those who claim to be either on the Left or Right.
Nothing getting done but a constant Fight.

If we follow the Laws and Rules from above.
It is known as Brotherly Love.

As you look around today,
it only makes you want to Pray.

There are those who continue lying.
As we stand by watching so many dying AND crying.

Frank J. Anderson

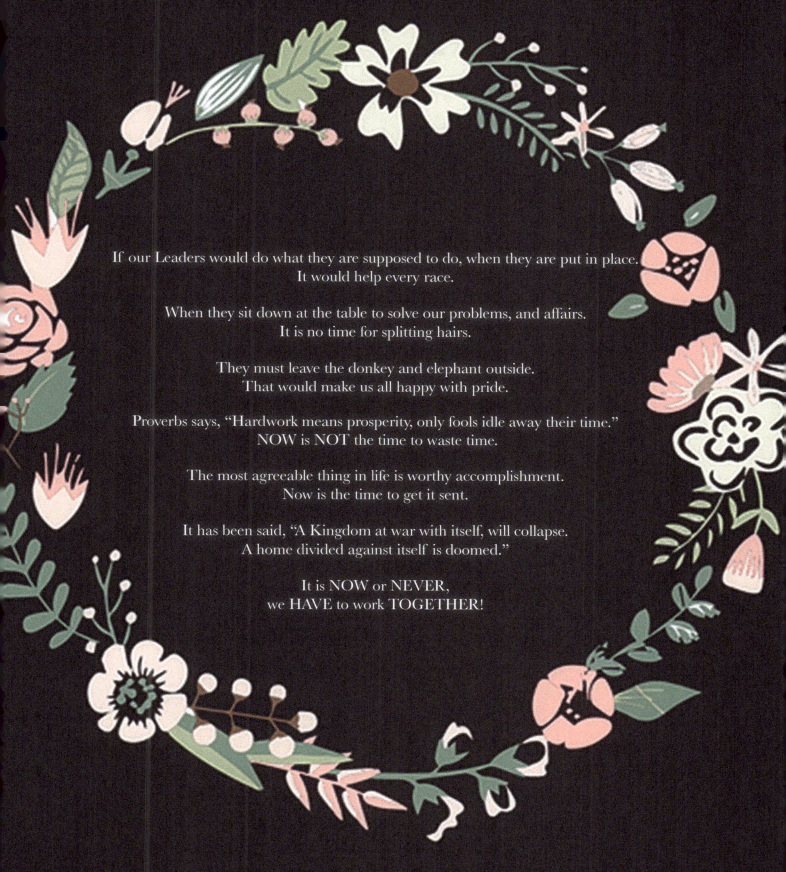

If our Leaders would do what they are supposed to do, when they are put in place.
It would help every race.

When they sit down at the table to solve our problems, and affairs.
It is no time for splitting hairs.

They must leave the donkey and elephant outside.
That would make us all happy with pride.

Proverbs says, "Hardwork means prosperity, only fools idle away their time."
NOW is NOT the time to waste time.

The most agreeable thing in life is worthy accomplishment.
Now is the time to get it sent.

It has been said, "A Kingdom at war with itself, will collapse.
A home divided against itself is doomed."

It is NOW or NEVER,
we HAVE to work TOGETHER!

Frank J. Anderson

Without a Doubt

By Frank J. Anderson
February 14, 2018

It has been said that roses are red,
and violets are blue
I can say that my heart is still in love with you
I have made promises to you in the past
I have strongly endeavored to make our love last
As we approach this Valentine's Day
I pray that our love will not go away
I know it has been difficult for you to hold on
For I have also tried to be strong
We have shared many years and many tears
Valentine's Day only comes once a year
I just want to say I will always be near
True love has no time frame
To let this go would be a shame
Love to you on Valentine's Day
My love is here to stay

To Moms & Pops
by Frank J. Anderson

This moment is dedicated to my Mother and Father.
Because my love is no greater for any others.

As I retrospect to days of the past, my only regret is that they did not last.
It is a joy to remember the wonderful days of past.

I took for granted you living from day to day.
I now have sadness and tears as I pray.

Not in my wildest imagination did I think that you would leave this world.
All my thoughts are in a whirl.

I miss you so dearly as you can see.
I know both of you are watching over me.

I accept the fact that you have gone to a better place than here.
We will always feel that you are near.

I hope you are proud as to what I have turned out to be.
I owe it all to thee.
I hope you know how much I loved you.
For my affection was genuine through and through.

As I travel this journey through the rest of my life,
I will always remember your advice.

Mom, I know you were happy to see "Pops" again to be with you.
But, without the both of you, we have to follow your advice, and that will see us through.

"Mom and Pops" we look forward to seeing you on the other side.
But until that time, we hope you will see US with pride.

Both of you were always my Best Friends.
You were always with me to the end.

Now it is my responsibility to step forward and take your place.
I promise you that I will NOT be a disgrace.

The things that you have taught me through the years,
I will always keep them close to me and dear.

God promised that we will meet again,
and that we will NEVER have a end.

Message from Dorothy to Me

Frank J. Anderson

Don't cry for me, my loves, I'm in Heaven above
My journey was fast
I was told early in life my stay on Earth would not last
Oh what a wonderful place to be and see
That's why I say don't cry for me
I brought all the love that each of you have given to me
Don't cry, my love, don't cry for me
I have spoken to God who promised
You will see me again
He said this was not the very end
You are still my best friend
It says in the Bible that "weeping may endure through the night
But joy comes in the morning"
During these times, you can use the wonderful gift of memory and prayer
That God gave each of us to communicate with me,
To communicate with me, there is no service fee,
The lines are never busy
You just close your eyes and you have a direct line to me
It is normal for you to be selfish in not wanting to lose me
But what you are witnessing today is God's will
We must let God take over from here
I ask that the love that we have shared with each other
Be passed onto all the sisters and brothers
As you and I can rejoice
In our personal moments together on Earth
I have many fond and class memories of each of you
Gone is the face you loved so dear
Silent is the voice you loved to hear
Too far away for sign or speech
But not too far for prayers to reach
Sweet to remember me as I was here
And now though am absent, am just as dear
May God continue to bless each of you in your endeavors
And Bless you until we meet again

Shepherd

by Frank J. Anderson

Pastor one of your jobs is to bring in the sheep.
So often when you get them in they fall asleep.

They can't get rid of their sin.
But you have to try to keep them in.

You have a very difficult task ahead of you.
But you are the man or woman that will see it through.

Some of your flock will go their separate way.
But you have promised God that you will stay.

You have been loyal to each of them through and through.
There is nothing else that you should do.

Keep bringing them in my friend.
God bless and amen.

For You and Me

by Frank J. Anderson

As a Nation and World, now is the time for our divisiveness and hate to pass.
Or, our Country and World will not last.

Our children are paying attention to what they hear and see.
When you look in the mirror, ask yourself is that me?
What they hear and see, is what they will be.

NOW is the time for each of us to concentrate, before it is too late.
In doing so, we don't need a lot of debate.

The time is NOW or NEVER!
Or we could be gone FOREVER!

Prayer, Life and Time

by Frank J. Anderson

Each day I pray and pray,
to make my trouble go away.

As I bend down on my knees and ask for relief,
It often test my spiritual belief.

I have heard so much app t what God can do.
But I am selfish and want to know when he will come through.

They say he is always on time.
I wonder when his time will be mine?

They tell me to be patient and I will see.
But patience is not a part of me.

How would you advise me to see my troubles through?
If you were me and not you.

No one can live my life the way I do,
No one could live my life the way I would want them to.

It's mine get your own....
Leave mine alone.

MESSAGE FROM ABOVE

BY FRANK J. ANDERSON

WRITTEN JANUARY 6, 2018

THERE WAS A CALL FROM ABOVE FOR YOU: "TUANITA"
THE MESSAGE WAS: I NEED YOU HERE MY LOVE.
YOU HAVE LABORED AND DONE ALL THE THINGS ON EARTH THAT I HAVE
ASKED YOU TO DO.
NOW IS THE TIME THAT YOUR WORK ON EARTH IS THROUGH.
THOSE ON EARTH WILL MISS YOU AS I HAVE CALLED YOU ABOVE.
THEY ARE ONLY EXPRESSING THEIR TRUE LOVE.
TUANITA, THOSE THAT YOU HAVE LEFT BEHIND,
WILL BE ABLE TO HAVE PEACE OF MIND
KNOWING THAT I HAVE YOU IN MY LOVING GRASP,
AND THIS IS NOT THE END, BUT ONLY THE PAST.
TUANITA, AS EACH OF US MOVES FORWARD FROM THIS DAY,
YOU HAVE LIVED AND SHOWN US THE PATH TO ETERNAL GRACE.
WE PROMISE THAT OUR ENDEAVORS TO GET THERE WILL NEVER CEASE.
AS YOU LOOK DOWN FROM ABOVE,
WE KNOW THAT WE HAVE YOUR CONTINUED LOVE.
AS DIFFICULT AS IT IS FOR US TO LET YOU GO,
WE MUST FOLLOW THE WORDS FROM GOD THAT WE KNOW.
WE ARE REMINDED THAT EVEN THOUGH YOU HAVE BEEN TAKEN AWAY,
THIS IS NOT THE END, WE WILL SEE YOU AGAIN ANOTHER DAY.
IT IS SAID THAT WEEPING MAY ENDURE THROUGH THE NIGHT,
BUT THAT JOY COMETH WITH THE MORNING LIGHT.
TUANITA, WE WILL ALL LOOK FORWARD TO THAT DAY.

IT HAS BEEN SAID OF YOU:
LIFE'S RACE WELL RUN
LIFE'S WORK WELL DONE
LIFE'S VICTORY RUN
NOW COMETH REST.

God's Gift

By Frank J. Anderson

September 1, 2018

On this very special, emotional day of my life
I thank God for letting me stay
As I stand before you, I want each of you to know
That much love, appreciation, and respect for you
Will never go away
I thank my wife and family
For always being by my side with pride
I hope that those that have gone before me
Can see that I am continuing to do my very best for thee
Lord, everything I have been to do
Could not have been accomplished without you
We are all living in a world and in our communities
That truly need love and change from each other
In order to live together as "Sister" and "Brother"
Dr. King, I agree with you
During the 80 years that God has given me
I have done my very best
It is up to God to let me finish the rest
And each of you have been apart of my success
In the future, I promise again to do my best
Until I am laid to rest
As we go forward from this day
I ask each of you to pray
That all the negative things in our lives will go away
Each of us can participate in making
A better world and community to live in
By accepting each other as equals as it was God's intent
Now is the time that we must live in peace
To make the world a better place and hate to cease
To each of you, thank you
For letting me be a part of your world
God's Gift is nothing new
He gave it with loving pride
To me and you

Things We Need To Do

By Frank J. Anderson

I know the history of where and how our Nation Begins.
But, I don't want to see it end.

There is a continued fight,
between those who claim to be either on the Left or Right.
Nothing getting done but a constant Fight.

If we follow the Laws and Rules from above.
It is known as Brotherly Love.

As you look around today,
it only makes you want to Pray.

There are those who continue lying.
As we stand by watching so many dying AND crying.

If our Leaders would do what they are supposed to do, when they are put in place.
It would help every race.

When they sit down at the table to solve our problems, and affairs.
It is no time for splitting hairs.

They must leave the donkey and elephant outside.
That would make us all happy with pride.

Proverbs says, "Hardwork means prosperity, only fools idle away their time."
NOW is NOT the time to waste time.

The most agreeable thing in life is worthy accomplishment.
Now is the time to get it sent.

It has been said, "A Kingdom at war with itself, will collapse.
A home divided against itself is doomed."

It is NOW or NEVER,
we HAVE to work TOGETHER!

Stay

by Frank J. Anderson

The first thing I do each day,
is wipe the obvious smile away.

A smile that only you can put on my face.
One that shines all over the place.

The thought of you makes my heart beat at a rapid pace.
It is those moments that is my saving grace.

When you talk about going away,
all I do is hope and pray, that you will stay.

I need you to remain with me, for I am a man who is in love, can't you see?
I hope that I can please you as you please me.

You are a part of me from way back when.
And will remain so until the very end.

Why I'm Telling You

by Frank J Anderson

The conversation that I am getting ready to have with you,
hopefully is about things I thought you knew.

It all begins with my Mental and Medical State.
I hope it's all before it's too late.

I have no plans of going away.
God only knows I want to stay.

The burdens that I find mindself in,
don't seem to want to end.

I asked God to Grant Me the Serenity to accept the things I cannot change,
the courage to change the things I can and the wisdom to know the difference.

When we complete our conversation,
I hope you will clearly understand my aggravation.

I asked God to see me through.
I don't know anything else to do.
THAT'S WHY I'M TELLING YOU.

Frank J. Anderson

Daddy's Poem

Daddy oh Daddy
Who knew, God would give me to you.
Daddy oh Daddy
What a Daddy so true

When God made me he gave me to you.
Someone to show how to live and what to do.

You know I love you and I am so proud.
I could shout and cheer and say it out loud.

So smart so loving and so brave.
Characters you will take to your grave.

You took the throw up, rides to school and life's mistakes.
You never left me out in the shade.

Just like the unknown, you never know it.
Just like Daddy, your daughter's a poet.

So with all my wishes from me to you.
DADDY I LOVE YOU.

Your loving daughter,
Franche'

We Need A Change
by Frank J. Anderson

Most of us people don't want to die and go away.
It's up to GOD how long we can stay.

The first thing we must do today,
is stop our bad habits and throw all hate away.

GOD knows we must stop the killing of each other.
He created us to be sisters and brothers and to love one another.

During this past several months, Mass Killings have been on the increase.
We are a World embarrassment, these horrible things must cease.

When a person takes the life of another person and rob them of love.
It violates all laws on Earth and Above.

The person who committed the sad situation,
did it without any hesitation.

May the victims rest in peace.
I pray to GOD for his relief.

Mass Killing Everywhere

by Frank J. Anderson
4/16/21

I truly believe in the 2nd Amendment.
But what happened in our city?
Today was not what the Amendment was intended to be.

These Mass Killings have happened here and other places before.
We don't need this to happen anymore.
It makes me wonder why they are knocking at the door.

There are too many people dying, and too many crying.
All along some are lying.

We continue to have killings all over the place.
Victims are made of all colors and race.

In the first three months of this year we've had three Mass Killings in our city.
What a shame and pity.

We have several months left in the year.
Are we gonna have to live in fear.

Eight people were killed in a mass killing yesterday.
Again we have to kneel and pray.

We must come together to solve this problem forever.
It is NOW or NEVER.

Domestic Situation

by Frank J. Anderson

Each time I have to take moments of my life to deal with stupidity.
Shortens my longevity.

Enough is enough. Let's end this stuff.
A gun in your hand, doesn't make you a man.

In order to survive,
you must give up the jive.

In the world that you have created,
is today overrated.

I truly understand your frustration.
But you must practice patience.

As you experience each day,
be aware that someone else paved your way.

As violence continues again and again.
It is up to you and I to make it end.

I know how you may feel,
but it does not give you a license to kill.

I feel your frustration,
but your violence is no justification.

If you are the the Daddy, don't let it end sadly.

The child that you brought in the world, whether a boy or girl.
What do you intend to do, to see it through?

Any fool can make a baby.
Are you a Father, maybe?

A Special Day For You

by Frank J. Anderson

My Dear Friend,

I regret that I was not physically able to be with you to celebrate your birthday. You have been present with me on several special times of my life.

Rest assure I am **always** with you in spirit.

The selection committee for your birthday said you passed with flying colors. Some of the testing was as followed:

1. You knew who you were when you looked in the mirror.
2. You went to the bathroom at least 7 times at night.
3. You remembered your name.
4. When getting dressed, you knew the left foot from the right foot.
5. You knew what day it was.
6. When communicating with others, your topic of conversation is about your aches and pains compared to theirs.
7. You can't find your keys, cell phone etc.
8. You forgot what you were getting ready to do.
9. Constantly asking people "what did you say?" while turning the volume up on everything.
10. Getting lost while driving.
11. Remembering to take your medicine and your doctor's appointments.

WELCOME to the WORLD of AGING!

How well you look at your age. I arrived at your age before you.

Boy what a trip through life has been, but this is not the end.

I'm so blessed that you are my friend. So dear to me, as close as a brother could be.

As we grew up together in life, we were faced with many challenges, the happy times and some sad. Through them all we were there supporting each other.

As we go forward together in this fourth quarter of life, I'm proud that we are still together on the same team of winners.

All I can say is Game ON!
Love you Brother!

Frank J. Anderson

For the Love of Payton
by Frank J. Anderson

There are some things I didn't get to say to Payton before he was called above. But he already knew he was my dear friend.

He was called above, where he has overwhelming love.
He was assured by God, that his work here on Earth was well done.
We all knew that Payton loved and was full of fun.
Over and over again, he was always there to help a friend.
During the times that he was not feeling his best.
He always stepped forward to help the rest.
When things were difficult for him to do, he always came forward to see them through.
Each of us may miss him as he was called from above.
We were only expressing our true love.
Those that he left behind, will be able to have a piece of mind. His special thoughts of love for his rock
Joan and brother Joe
knowing that he has you in his loving heart, your memories will never be apart.
As he looks down from above, he knows that he has each of your continued love.
As difficult as it is for you to let him go, we must follow the words from God that we know.
We are reminded that even though Payton has been called home, it is with
his loving memories that won't leave us alone.
During these times, that we should miss you, we will use the memories to reminisce of you.
This is not the end, we will see Payton again.

God's word says, "Weeping may endure for a night, but joy comes in the morning."
We all look forward to that day.

Frank J. Anderson

Quotes & Shorts

By Frank J. Anderson

Think Before You Speak

Sometimes the words that come out of our mouths, should be filtered through an element of common sense.
For some, that filtration is late, that's what brings about hate.

Reflection

"When you are blaming people for mistakes that have been made, don't forget to look in the mirror."

No Rest for the Diligent

"Sleep is good and necessary for the body, but during that time NO task can be completed."

Vision

"The things you see with your eyes may not be what it really is, people included."

Life

When a person goes through life, they have "good days" and "bad days." But the best days are the "ALIVE days."

Leave the Door Open

Through all the things I have achieved. I didn't do it to be the first **black** to accomplish that goal.
I always thought about those who came before me and what struggles they went through to open the door for me.
I will always keep my foot in the door to keep it open for others who are deserving and qualified to achieve their goal.

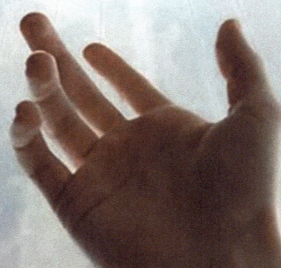

Frank J. Anderson

Called Home

by Frank J. Anderson

To each of my loved ones, I have been called to come above.
I can assure each of you, that I carried each of your love.

It was as difficult for me as it was for you.
God has promised that we will see this through.

This is not the end. We will see each other again.

No Left, No Right Only Peace Without A Fight

by Frank J. Anderson

If we don't get together,
there will be no peace forever.

It is easy for so many to say, I support the left or right.
Most times it ends up in a vicious fight.

Let us make sure that the decisions we make,
don't end up as a mistake.

All the Laws that are being passed,
makes one wonder if our Nation will last.

A single act of working together,
could make us last forever.

Your Choice

by Frank J. Anderson

Over and over again, I thought you were my friend.
But the things you do and say, make me want to walk away.
You are embarrassing me with your continued harassing of others.

Others continue to complain about you and me together.
This relationship cannot last forever.

The time of our relationship is ticking away.
You have to make major changes for me to stay.

Frank J. Anderson

Stop the Killings
by Frank J. Anderson

Enough is enough! Of this killing stuff!

To kill another is a 111ajor sin, we must bring to an end.
To kill another whatever the reason may be,
has no logical reason that we can see.

To kill a mass group of people because they are not your equal, or
for a hate is STILL a sin.
May they rest in Peace, this stuff MUST end!

We pray for God's relief and ending of this sin.
We need to work together, to stop this sin forever, Amen.

Frank J. Anderson

One for Me
by Frank J. Anderson

If it were not for you,
I know that my love life would be through.

With the rise each day of the sun,
I know that my love will continue on.

With the setting of the sun at the end of each day,
Does not mean that our love will go away.

My dear love it is no doubt you came from above.
You are as precious to me as a loving dove.

I long for you each minute of the day.
I will never let that feeling go away.
I look forward to loving you each day.

As time goes by you will see,
you will always be the one for me.

Frank J. Anderson

What America Needs from Me & You
by Frank J. Anderson

As we get older and older,
hate and divisiveness gets bolder and bolder.

One of the things that we as adults continue to do,
is to pass on to our children by what we say and do.

They want to be like you and me.
They follow what they hear and see.
The results is what they will be.

Each of us ended in this country under different ways.
Different times and different days.

Many in search of hope,
others by rope.

Where are we today?
We need help along the way.

The leaders that we are selecting today,
we need to be aware of who they are and what they say.

God did not make all of us the same.
We should not use that as blame.

The bible says. "A Nation at war with itself, will collapse.
A home divided against itself is doomed."

I'm ready, where are you?
I extend my hand to you.
WE can see our Nation through.

Frank J. Anderson

We Need Change

by Frank J Anderson
April 20, 2021

I've been in the law arena for approximately 60 years.
I've seen happiness and a lot of tears.

I've seen life and death throughout my career.
The ugliness and hate was always near.

My life was always at risk,
but I continued to do this.

My Goal was to make things better.
That was my true endeavor.

Many things I can't forget.
We have no solution for them yet.

In a court today,
there was a decision that hopefully take hate away.

My brother's name is George, and my best friend's name was Floyd
Today George Floyd's name rang around the world without void.

Upon his death, his little girl said, "My Daddy changed the world."
Which forever changed HER world.

The decision that was made in court today, will hopefully take some hate away.
From the bottom of my heart I pray.

Is This You?

by by Frank J Anderson

Here we go again as we awake.
To find a continuation to experience Racial hate.

Enough is enough of this Earthly sin.
When will this ugliness end.

So many crying, so many dying.
So many people *lying*.

There are many who want to put a stop to this.
There are more who want to continue to resist.

Where do you fit into this mess?
Your daily actions are your test.

Do you stand by and become a participant in spreading hate or as an eyewitness
to victim of hate to others?
Are you strong enough to step in and protect your God given Sisters or Brothers?

God created each and every one of us, who are you to make a fuss over his creations.
What he put together is the start of Worlds and Nations.

People of all different sizes and colors.
Not all looking like the others.

What their children hear and see.
ls what they will be.

Now it's time for all of us to make a change to accept each other,
as our God given Sisters and Brothers.

If we don't stop our hateful ways,
we will surely end our living days.

ls this YOU?
What are YOU going to do?

Frank J. Anderson

America What's Going On?
by Frank J. Anderson

Marvin Gaye wrote a song about it.
The song continues to be a hit.
But we still don't have a answer to it

We continue to get more divided.
Many want to ignore and hide the answer to it.

In many cases, it has something to do with hate or races.

Most of us want to live and get along with each other.
Their our God given sisters and brothers.

But many continue to kill.
Going against God's will.

What's going on in my people's heart, Is what is keeping our Nation apart.

Frank J. Anderson

It's been said, "A Kingdom at war within itself will collapse. A home divided against itself is doomed."

It is now or never. We have to live and work together.

One thing we can do as adults to answer "What's Going On?", is be mindful
of what we say and do in the presence of our children.

What you say and do, will make them want to be like you.

There are those who are appointed to be leaders
In reality, they turn out to be non-achievers.

Killing of individuals, and in mass,
is a sad state of affairs that can't continue to last.

That's what's going on, and can't let it last.
Now is the time for us to fix "What's Going On?" or we will all be of the past.

Father's Day

by Frank J. Anderson

Today is Father's Day even though My Pops has gone above.

MY love for him will never cease.
He is with God where he will have everlasting Peace.

Pops since you have been gone,
Everything in the world seem to have gone wrong.

You taught me to love and respect my God sent sisters and brothers.
So many people are killing each other.
Because they don't look like one another.

To each Father on this day:
Be mindful of what you do and say in the presence of your children.
what they hear and see in you, makes them want to be like you.

The presence of hate is at an all time high.
We need to pray that it will die.

Many Fathers are no longer with us on this day, due to hate.
Hate has taken them away as we celebrate this day.

As time moves forward there will be, more Fathers to be.
Pops I thank God for giving you to me.

I hope I am doing what you told me to do,
treat others as you want them to treat you.

As we celebrate this day,
Pops, my love for you will never go away.
My love for you will never end,
with Faith and Love we will see each other again.

My Sister Joyce

by Frank J Anderson

Today we celebrate your 80th Birthday with Love.
We bring you blessings from God above.

As I look back on the many years that you've been my God sent
Sister from above,
You arrived with everlasting love.

Our lives have traveled together with everlasting respect and love
for each other.
That's why you are my Sister and I am your Brother.

I may be older than you,
but I will endeavor to always be there for you.

There have been good days and sad days in the past.
But God's gift to both of us has let us last.

On this day we both thank God for bring us together.
I will love you forever.

Your Brother Frank.

We Need You

by Frank J Anderson

I've given my best when I took the 60 year Law Enforcement Test given by each of you.
Today I have no regrets, hopefully neither do you.
I have had many Good days, Bad days and Sad days.
Each day all if these are the emotions that Law Enforcement takes you through.
Would I do it again? I would love to start over again without hesitation.
But I can only have dreams of my past in my personal meditation.

And hope they will last. The reminiscent past.

As I took forward to our Law Enforcement Society Work today, I'm somewhat concerned as to what I see and hear.
So many people killed by hate and fear.

So many of our Law Enforcement Brothers and Sisters have been killed, some giving up and quit due to lack of support.

As we move forward we must learn to live with and respect our God sent Sisters and Brothers,
even though we don't look like one another.

For those who are in Elected positions,
you must leave the Donkey and Elephant outside the room and do what is best for ALL of the people you represent when making decisions.

We are going to need to replace those who are no longer in Law Enforcement for whatever reason.
I am thankful for my 60 years season.

I encourage all qualified persons to step forward and join the ranks of Law Enforcement, I DID 60 years ago.
Our Country, State and Communities need you.
I DID IT, and so CAN YOU!
****BY THE WAY SHERIFF FORESTALL IS HIRING TODAY!****

Frank J. Anderson

Warning From Above

by Frank J Anderson

Wild fires erupting in the West.
Washing D.C. in a terrible mess.

There is a message being sent to all.
But most people are not paying attention to the awakening call

Each day and every day that we look the other way,
only brings us closer to our dooming day.

If we continue down this path,
we will surely run out of gas.

The promise that has come from above,
only comes true with Brotherly Love.

Wake up people, the message has been sent.
It is time for all of us to repent.

Our lives are so inundated with hatred and blame.
We should all be ashamed.

Frank J. Anderson

Letter to My Wife

December 28, 2019

Dear Mert:

As we celebrate our 56th wedding anniversary on this day.

we can both attest that we have been through heaven and hell on our way to this day.

But I'm here to say it was worth the trip.

would l do it again, yes without a thought or a doubt or mental reservation. I have endeavored to be a good husband, but I'm still a "work in process"

I'm not as sharp and strong as I use to be, but I'm always up for the challenge to get things done.
we both need to work on our communication skills/problem.
I think hearing aids "could be a big help sometimes for each of us to understand what the other said or is saying.

As we venture thru the upcoming years, we should have no fears.

Our love and affection that we have shared with each other, will survive us through challenges ahead.

I know that you have made many personal sacrifices thru the many years in keeping our family together during, my absence in following the career path that I chose to follow.

We have been blessed with children, grandchildren and great grandchildren. I hope and have endeavored, that as the leader of our family, I have each of their love and respect.

Frank J. Anderson

God willing, I look forward to continuing in this role. As I started, I'm still a "work in process"

To each of you who are with us on this 56yr. celebration. Thank you,

We consider each of you a part of our foundation.

To the children, we have endeavored to prepare you with love and affection and

the necessary tools to be successful in life and decent people.

You are still a "work in progress"

We will continue to be there for you when needed, God willing

To my wife, I have made promises to you in the past.

This one, I will strongly endeavore to make our love last.

I know it has been difficult for you to hold on for so long.

For I have also tried to be strong.

We have shared many years and tears together.

I promise that my love is forever

True love has no time frame.

This is not the end of the game.

I say "Game On"

Love Always,
Frank

Frank J. Anderson

Let Hate Be Gone

by Frank J Anderson

Hate is getting worse and worse each day.
It seems as though it just doesn't want to go away.

Over and over I pray for hate to go away.
I need others to help me pray for that day.

Each day that hate is around.
Continues to bring our World and Nation down.

We must all be aware of what we say and do in the company of our
children, if your actions are negative about others.

Because what they hear and see you do,
they will want to be like you.

Even though we don't all look like each other,
WE are ALL God sent sisters and brothers.

NOW is the time to STOP hate,
Before it's TOO LATE!

Frank J. Anderson

To Our Elected Officials-09/25/21
by Frank J Anderson

What are you doing to bring our Nation together?
We cannot stay divided forever,
on decisions you must make.
Our Democracy is at stake,
we can't afford to make a mistake.

Regardless of your political affiliation,
we cannot afford to lose our Democracy and Nation.
The decisions you make on issues must be in the best interest of those you
were elected to represent.
That is why you were sent.

As you come and meet together,
your decisions will follow you forever.

Park the elephant and donkey outside.
Then you can do your job with pride.

We Need All Hands On Deck

By Frank J Anderson
09/25/21

We continue to conquer space,
but what we have done to Earth is a disgrace.

I don't know where to begin.
But I hope this is not the end.

As we look around each day,
hate won't go away.

We continue to receive and ignore warning signs from above.
Fires, floods, droughts, virus and the lack of love for each other.

We have turned this beautiful world that was given to us by God above,
into a place of hate and the lack of love.

Where do we go from here?
Seek love and have no fear.

Our world is headed for a shameful wreck
so where are we going, what the heck!

If we continue the course we are on,
surely our world will be gone. ☹

Frank J. Anderson

Red White and Blue-

A Message to You-09/26/21

by Frank J Anderson

We have a lot of work to do.
There are the colors of our flag, red white and blue.

Our nation was built on the principle of acceptance to everyone regardless
of race, creed or color.
Accepting and respecting one another.

Unfortunately many don't support that principle of our ancestors.
To live and love one another.

What a great thing about the red, white and blue.
It opened the door for me and you.

As we sing the "Star-Spangled Banner"
Let us accept ALL brothers and sisters in a loving manner.

CPSIA information can be obtained
at www.ICGtesting.com
Printed in the USA
BVHW020022190522
637306BV00007BA/28